IT'S TIME TO LEARN ABOUT BASSET HOUNDS

It's Time to Learn about Basset Hounds

Walter the Educator

Silent King Books
A WhichHead Entertainment Imprint

Copyright © 2025 by Walter the Educator

All rights reserved. No part of this book may be reproduced in any manner whatsoever without written per- mission except in the case of brief quotations embodied in critical articles and reviews.

First Printing, 2024

Disclaimer

This book is a literary work; the story is not about specific persons, locations, situations, and/or circumstances unless mentioned in a historical context. Any resemblance to real persons, locations, situations, and/or circumstances is coincidental. This book is for entertainment and informational purposes only. The author and publisher offer this information without warranties expressed or implied. No matter the grounds, neither the author nor the publisher will be accountable for any losses, injuries, or other damages caused by the reader's use of this book. The use of this book acknowledges an understanding and acceptance of this disclaimer.

It's Time to Learn about Basset Hounds is a collectible early learning book by Walter the Educator suitable for all ages belonging to Walter the Educator's Time to Eat Book Series. Collect more books at WaltertheEducator.com

USE THE EXTRA SPACE TO TAKE NOTES AND DOCUMENT YOUR MEMORIES

BASSET HOUNDS

With floppy ears and legs so short,

It's Time to Learn about
Basset Hounds

The Basset Hound is of a sort

A dog that sniffs both low and wide,

With nose to ground and tail with pride.

Their bodies long, their voices deep,

They love to howl, they love to sleep!

With wrinkled skin and droopy eyes,

They look so sad, but they're so wise!

A Basset's nose is strong and true,

They smell things far away from view.

No tiny scent will pass them by,

They track with noses held up high!

They walk so slow, but don't be fooled,

Their hunting skills are finely schooled.

They sniff and search and never quit,

Until they find the perfect fit!

It's Time to Learn about
Basset Hounds

They're friendly dogs who love to play,

.

But sometimes they will stray away.

If sniffing leads them down a trail,

They may not hear you when you wail!

With loving hearts and gentle ways,

They'll be your friend for all your days.

A loyal hound with love so true,

A Basset Hound will stick with you!

They love their food, oh yes, they do,

And sometimes beg for extra, too!

But keep them fit and help them run,

So they stay strong and full of fun!

Their ears are long, they drag and sway,

They pick up scents along the way.

So keep them clean and wipe them well,

It's Time to Learn about
Basset Hounds

Or they might start to have a smell!

They nap a lot, they take their time,

But when they play, they shine and climb!

They love a walk, a sniff, a treat,

And curling up beside your feet.

So if you see a Basset Hound,

With floppy ears that touch the ground,

Just know they're kind and love you true,

It's Time to Learn about
Basset Hounds

And they would love a hug from you!

ABOUT THE CREATOR

Walter the Educator is one of the pseudonyms for Walter Anderson. Formally educated in Chemistry, Business, and Education, he is an educator, an author, a diverse entrepreneur, and he is the son of a disabled war veteran. "Walter the Educator" shares his time between educating and creating. He holds interests and owns several creative projects that entertain, enlighten, enhance, and educate, hoping to inspire and motivate you. Follow, find new works, and stay up to date with Walter the Educator™

at WaltertheEducator.com